I0012297

A PRACTICAL, PROJECT-BASED

INTRODUCTION TO PYTHON

PROGRAMMING.

Contents

4

COPYRIGHT CLAIM

This book is owned by Professor Touceef who works as assistant professor at associate college.

Forward
Describe Python.

Python is a well-known general-purpose cloud computer language with a wide range of uses. It is ideal for both scripting or "glue code" that links components as well as the creation of sophisticated programs due to its high-level data structures, dynamic typing, variable binding, and a plethora of other capabilities. Additionally, it could be enhanced such that practically any operating system could execute C or C++ applications and call system functions. Python is a universal language that may be used in a wide range of applications and is compatible with almost any system architecture.

Python is an object-oriented, interpretive programming language. Classes, dynamic typing, extremely high level dynamic data types, exceptions, modules, and exception handling are among the characteristics listed.

The Python Packaging Index (PyPI) hosts hundreds of third-party modules for the computer language. For example, Django is a prominent standard for web development, while NumPy, Pandas, and Mathplotlib are well-known standards for data research.

History of Python

Popular high-level, all-purpose programming language Python. It was first developed by Guido van Rossum, then by the Python Software Foundation. Thanks to its emphasis on code readability, programmers may convey ideas using its syntax and less lines of code.

It was going to be the late 1980s when history was written. Python development started at that point. Guido Van Rossum soon after began working on application-based projects at the Netherlands-based Centrum Wiskunde & Informatics (CWI) in December 1989. He first started it as a hobby project since he was looking for something entertaining to do during the holidays. The ABC Programming

Language, which Python is credited for outperforming, included exception handling and interacted with the Amoeba Operating System. In the beginning of his career, he had helped to establish ABC. Although he had seen certain issues with ABC, he generally liked its features. The next action he took was really rather wise. He had included some of the beneficial elements and syntax of ABC. He totally addressed those issues and created a powerful scripting language that was faultless as a result of the feedback it received. He named it Python because he was a huge fan of the BBC television show "Monty Python's Flying Circus" and wanted a catchy, memorable, and somewhat intriguing name for his invention. Up until his resignation as leader on

July 12th, 2018, he presided as the "Benevolent dictator for life" (BDFL). He used to work for Google for a time, but right now he works for Drop box. In 1991, the language was eventually made public. When compared to Java, C++, and C, it required a lot less code to describe the concepts when it was first published. Its design ethos was also extremely sound. Its primary goals are to improve developer efficiency and code readability. When it was first introduced, it had more than enough power to provide classes with inheritance, a number of fundamental data types, exception handling, and functions.

Putting Python into Windows

Python may be installed on a Windows computer in a variety of methods. The choices we'll investigate in this lesson are listed below:

Installing Python straight from the Microsoft Store is a fast and simple alternative that will have you using Python in no time. Beginners who wish to use Python on their computer for learning reasons will find it extremely helpful.

Directly downloading Python that extends from the Python website: With this approach, you have greater control over the installation procedure and may personalize your installation.

Using an Anaconda distribution, install Python: A well-liked Python installation called Anaconda has a lot of pre-installed tools and packages, making it a suitable choice for scientific computing and data research.

Whichever approach you choose with, it won't take you long to have Python running on your Windows computer. On occasion, your computer may come pre-installed with Python. Here's how to check whether Python is installed on your Windows computer.

Identifying Python Installations on Windows Machines

Both the Start Menu and the terminal may be used to access Python.

You may use the terminal to check whether Python is set up on your Windows computer by doing the following steps:

Open a command-line program, such as Command Prompt (the default in Windows 10 or Windows 11) or Windows Terminal.

'Python' should be typed into the command line. If Python is set up, a message similar to "Python 3.x.x" should appear, followed by the Python prompt, which is shown as ">>>". Keep in mind that Python's version number is "3.x.x".

You will be directed immediately to the Python installation in the Microsoft Store if Python is not already installed on your computer. Please be aware that Python may not be updated on the page you are going to.

Set up Python

Open the downloaded package to launch the installation.

Accepting the default install location is secure, and adding Python to PATH is essential. Python apps, which need Python to function, won't know where to locate it if you don't add it to your PATH environment variable. Before continue, enable this option at the bottom of the install window as it is not already chosen.

You must give Windows your consent before it will let you install an application via a publisher other than Microsoft. When the User Account Control panel asks you to, click yes.

When Windows has completed distributing the files from the Python package to the relevant places, wait patiently until it is finished. At that point, Python installation is complete.

Time to have fun.

Set up an IDE

Although a text editor is all you truly need to construct Python programs, having an integrated development environment (IDE) is useful. A text editor with several user-friendly and practical Python capabilities is integrated into an IDE. Two excellent open source choices to take into consideration are IDLE 3 and Pycharm (Community Edition).

IDLE 3

An IDE named IDLE is included with Python. You may write code in any text editor, but utilizing an IDE gives you access to features like keyword highlighting to help you spot errors, a Run button to quickly and easily test your code, and other tools that are often not available in basic text editors like Notepad++.

Click the Start (or Window) menu and search for matches for "python" to launch IDLE. Since Python offers several interfaces, you could discover a few matches, so be sure to start IDLE.

Your Initial Program

"Hello, World!" is a timeless example of a first program. Let's follow convention. Enter after entering the following:

"Hello, World!" is printed.
The world can now be at your fingertips, even if it may not seem like much. Say hello one again. Join us for the next lecture on executing and saving files in IDLE.

Data Formats

Variables in Python may store values of several data kinds, sometimes referred to as value types. The most typical data kinds are as follows:

- Whole numbers such as 1, 2, and 3 are known as integers (int).
- Floats: Decimal numbers like 3, 14, 2, 718, and 1.61 80 339
- (str) Strings character sequences like "hello" and "world"
- (bool) Booleans: True or False values for logic
- The type() method may be used to determine the type of a variable:

- print(type(x)) # prints cl x = 5

Integers

Effectively, there is no length restriction on integer values in Python 3. As with anything else, it is obviously limited by the RAM available on your machine, but otherwise, an integer may be as long as you need it to be:

```
>>>                          print
(12312312312312312312312312 3
123123123123123123123   +   1)
12312312312312312312312312 3
123123123123123123124
```

Python considers the following sequence of decimal digits to be a decimal number:

```
>>> print(10)
10
```

Creating Parameters

In Python, you could lead to a new variable by assigning a value to an existing one using the assignment operator (=). The variable name may be any combination of letters, digits, and underscores, but a number cannot be the first character. Here are some examples of how Python variables have been used:

Z equals 3.14 when x = 5 and y = "Hello World"
Additionally, you may assign a lot of variables at once:

When x, y, and z are equal to 5, the message "Hello World" appears.
When naming variables in Python, adhering to a few principles is essential. Variable names should be descriptive and lowercase (snake case), and words should be separated by underscores. Variable_name is a better name than VariableName or variablename. Additionally, Python has a few words that cannot be used as variable names, like if, else, True, False, None, and, or, not, etc.

Shifting variables

After a variable has been established, its value may be changed by assigning it a new one. For illustration:

x = 5 x = 10

In the previous example, x is first set to 5, and subsequently its value is changed to 10.

Strings

Sequences of characters make up strings. In Python, the string type is known as str.

Single or double quotes may be used to separate string literals. The string includes every character between the creation delimiter and the corresponding closing delimiter:

>>> Printing "I am a string."

I'm just a string.
type ("I am a string.")
'str' class="">

>>> print("I'm with you.")
I concur.
>>> type("I'm with you.") class'str'>
In Python, a string may have any number of characters. Your computer's RAM resources are the sole restriction. Also possible is an empty string:

>>> " '"

String Escape Sequences

Python may be asked to read a character or group of characters inside a string in multiple ways on occasion. One of two things might lead to this:

You may wish to turn off the unique interpretation that certain characters in a string often get.

You may wish to give letters in a string that are often considered literally a particular meaning.

This may be done by inserting a backslash () character. In a string, a backslash character denotes that one or more characters should be given special treatment. The backslash causes the next character sequence to "escape" its regular meaning, which is why this is known as an escape sequence.

Let's see how this works.

Which five arithmetic procedures are there?

Multiplication * Multiplies one operand by the other Division / Divides the first operand by the second Addition + Adds one operand to the other Subtraction - Subtracts the second operand from the first

Modulo % returns the remainder after dividing the first and second INTEGER operands.

Commentary: What are they and how do they work in Python?

Lines of code marked with a comment in Python are disregarded by the interpreter when the program runs. Programmers may better comprehend a piece of code by adding comments that make it simpler to read. Just one line may be used for comments in Python,

25

which supports three different types.

What are Python's three conditional statements?

Examples of If Statements in Python: How to Use Conditional...
The basic building blocks of programming are conditional statements (if, else, and elif), which let you direct the course of your program in response to certain situations. They provide you a means to make choices inside your program and have other code run depending on those choices. In Python, how do you build an if/elif/else conditional?

IF...ELIF...ELSE Python Statements

Example. #!/usr/bin/python var = 100 When var equals 200, print Printing "1 - Got a true expression value" if var is greater than or equal to 150.elif var == 100: print "3 - Got a true expression value" print var else: print "4 - Got a false expression value" print var print "Goodbye!" print var print "2 - Got a true expression value"

What do Python for loops achieve?

A piece of code may be repeated a certain number of times using for loops. For-loops are often used with inerrable objects like lists and ranges. The block is carried out each time a Python for express iterates through the elements in a sequence in chronological order.

In Python Pharm, how do you indent a piece of code?

Press Ctrl Alt 0I while in the editor to select the required code piece. Go to Editor | Code Style in the Settings menu (Ctrl Alt 0S) if you need to change the indentation settings. Select the necessary indents choices on the Tabs and Indents tab of the relevant language page, and then click OK.

Python should indent by two or four spaces.

The language does not specify the amount of indentation in a level, therefore it might vary from one block to the next. However, each block must be indented by one level in relation to the one before it. The interpreter is content as long as each block is consistent. We usually utilize four slots per level as a norm.

Reasoning operators

Logic operators (either True or False) are used to conditional expressions in Python. They carry out operations such as logical AND, logical OR, and logical NOT.

OPERATOR DESCRIPTION LOGICAL AND SYNTAX AND: True if both the operands (x, y), or logical, are true.

OR: If either of the operands (x or y) is true, then the result is true. NOT: If the operand is not x, it is true.

Python error handling

The try block allows you to check a block of code for errors.

The unless block may be used to fix the error.

You may still execute code by using the finally block, regardless of the results of the try- and except blocks.

Handling of instances

Python often terminates and outputs an error message in the case of an error, or exception as we call it.

Some exceptions may be handled with the try statement:

Example Spend money on a Python server.

The try block will result in the exception being triggered since x is not specified:

Try printing x without the phrase "An exception occurred"
Since the try block generated an error, the except block will be executed.

Without the try block, the program will incorrectly crash and provide an error message:

Example
This assertion cannot be true since x is not defined:

print(x)

What does Python file management entail?

In addition to Create, Open, Append, Read, and Write, Python also supports...

In programming, dealing with files is a regular task. Python's built-in methods for generating, opening, and closing files make managing files easier. While a file is open, Python also enables a variety of file actions, such as reading, writing, and appending data.

What are the Python file operations?

1. Use the open () method in Python to open a file in the "r" mode, which indicates that it is only available for reading.

The mode 'w' indicates that the file is solely accessible for writing.

The output of that program will be appended to the previous output of that file, as indicated by the mode 'a'.

Modules for Python

Starting by grouping similar code is a smart option if you would like your code to be nicely structured. A module is essentially a group of related lines of code stored in a.py file. In a module, you may decide whether to define variables, classes, or functions. Runnable code may be included in modules without issue.

Let's write a function, for instance, to welcome new students to a certain course:

Print def. welcome message (course)("We appreciate your interest in our " + course + " course. Soon, you'll get an email with all the information.

We save this code in a file called welcome.py so that it may be included in the welcome module.

We must first import the appropriate module using the import line before we can utilize this code in our application. Then, by invoking the function with the module, we will be prepared to utilize a function specified in this module. Syntax for function ():

Welcome import welcome. "Python Basics Part 1" welcome message
Output
We appreciate your interest in taking our Python Basics Part 1 course. Soon, you'll get an email with all the information.

Packages for Python

You could create a lot of diverse, challenging-to-manage modules while creating a big application. You'll gain by grouping and structuring your modules in this situation. Packages come into play at that point.

In essence, Python packages are collections of modules in a directory. The module namespace's hierarchical structure is supported by packages. We may arrange our modules into packages and sub packages in the same way that we arrange our data on a hard drive into directories and subfolders.

A directory must have the file __init__.py for it to be regarded as a package (or sub package). The initialization code for the related package is often included in this file.

For instance, we may put the modules for our data science project in the package my model, as seen below:

Python modules, packages, libraries, and frameworks have different properties.
Using the dot notation, we may import certain modules from this package. One of the following code snippets, for instance, may be used to import the dataset module from the aforementioned package:

The dataset for my model's training

What are Classes und Objects in Python Object-Oriented Programming?

In order to build objects, Python, like every other object-oriented language, lets you declare classes. The most popular data types in Python, such strings, lists, dictionaries, and so on, are built-in Python classes.

A class defines a certain object type via a group of related methods and instance variables. A class may be compared to the model or blueprint of an item. The terms assigned to the variables that make up a class are called attributes.

An object is an instance of a class with a specified set of attributes. As a consequence, an unlimited number of objects may be created using the same class.

Let's create a class called Book for the sales software used by booksellers.

Self. Title = title self. Quantity = quantity class Book: def __init__(self, title, quantity, author, price)
Self. Author equals author self. Price equals cost

What distinguishes scripting from programming?

Programming languages are used to create huge, complicated software applications like operating systems and enterprise-level software, while scripting languages are used for simpler jobs. They are also used in the creation of system utilities and device drivers, which are lower-level pieces of software.

PEP8 coding style: what is it?

Using PEP 8, Learn to Write Stunning Python Code - True Python

PEP 8 recommends capping lines to 79 characters. This is due to the fact that it enables simultaneous opening of several files and prevents line wrapping. Of course, it's not always practical to limit assertions to 79 characters or fewer. Methods for allowing statements to span several lines are described in PEP 8.

What is a code's readability?

The first is that the code must provide the anticipated result, and the second is that it must be simple for other developers to comprehend. These are the two main criteria for code readability. Clean code is like a clean coffee cup; if it's dirty, nobody will want to clean it for you so that you may use it.

Why use tools for debugging?

When mistakes happen, it might be difficult to identify and fix the problem. The use of debugging tools and techniques speeds up issue resolution and increases developer output. As a consequence, both the quality of the program and the end-user experience are enhanced.

What are the four debugging steps?

Two carefully monitored student trials revealed a four-step debugging behavior model: Understanding the system, testing it, finding the issue, and fixing it are the first three steps.

Who typically develops and runs unit tests?

Developers

As they are written as code that sits in the codebase alongside the application code they are testing, unit tests are often generated by developers during the development phase of a project. There are several frameworks for managing and executing unit tests that developers may use.

Is Python used for web development or data science?

Learning Python for Web Development vs. Python for Data Science Python programming for web development necessitates that programmers become proficient with a variety of web frameworks, such as Django, that can assist them in creating websites, whereas learning Python for data science necessitates that data scientists become proficient with regular expressions, begin using scientific libraries, and master the data.

What are the top 5 Python principles for data science that you need to know today?

Python Data Science: 5 Key Ideas You Should Understand...

Python Data Science: 5 Key Ideas You Should Understand Now, Big Data, AI, Machine Learning, Databases, and Programming.

Where is the Python community located?

On the website discuss.python.org, you can find the official Pi Community forums. Please visit the Python Wiki's local community's page if you're seeking for more forums or boards in your native tongue.